Nelson Thornes **Framework English**

Skills in **Grammar** and **Style**

Geoff Reilly

Series Consultant: **John Jackman**

Published in 2004 by:
Nelson Thornes Ltd
Delta Place
27 Bath Road
CHELTENHAM
GL53 7TH
United Kingdom

04 05 06 07 08 / 10 9 8 7 6 5 4 3 2 1

A catalogue record for this book is available from the British Library

ISBN 0 7487 7794 6

Illustrations by Richard Morris, Angela Lumley and Bill Piggins
Design, photo compositing and page make-up by Viners Wood Associates

Printed in Croatia by Zrinski

Acknowledgements
Corbis, p.16, p.22, p.30, p.44; Corbis GS (NT), p.34; Corel 18 (NT), p.26; Corel 62 (NT), p.56; Corel 251 (NT), p.38; Corel 350 (NT), p.4; Corel 387 (NT), p.20; Corel 664 (NT), p.18; Corel 676 (NT), p.10; Corel 740 (NT), p.14; Corel 750 (NT), p.58; Corel 778 (NT), p.48; Digital Vision 15 (NT), p.54, p.60; Peter Adams/Digital Vision BP (NT), p.42; Digital Vision KS (NT), p.72; John Foxx (NT), p.12 Photodisc 41 (NT), p.46; Photodisc 46 (NT), p.76; Photodisc 51 (NT), p.32; Photodisc 59 (NT), p.40; Photodisc 73 (NT), p.8.

CONTENTS

Topic

1	Main and subordinate clauses 1	4
2	Main and subordinate clauses 2	6
3	Noun clauses	8
4	Adjectival clauses	10
5	Adverbial clauses	12
6	Relative clauses	14
7	Punctuation of quoted (direct) speech	16
8	Reported (indirect) speech	18
9	Sentence types	20
10	Subject and predicate	22
11	Direct and indirect object	24
12	Subject-verb agreement	26

CHECK-UP 1 (Topics 1–12) — 28

13	Simple sentences	30
14	Compound sentences	32
15	Complex sentences	34
16	Negatives and double negatives	36
17	Active and passive voice	38
18	Sentence variety 1	40
19	Sentence variety 2	42
20	Sentence variety 3	44
21	Sentence beginnings 1	46
22	Sentence beginnings 2	48
23	Sentence transitions	50

CHECK-UP 2 (Topics 13–23) — 52

24	Paragraphs 1	54
25	Paragraphs 2	56
26	Paragraphs 3	58
27	Paragraphs 4	60
28	The basic essay: flow diagram	62
29	The basic essay: outline	64
30	The basic essay: introduction	66
31	The basic essay: body paragraphs	68
32	The basic essay: conclusion	70
33	The basic essay: narratives	72
34	Style	74
35	Style devices and tone	76

CHECK-UP 3 (Topics 24–35) — 78

MAIN AND SUBORDINATE CLAUSES 1

Clauses are small groups of words similar to phrases, except that **clauses** contain a verb, eg

The girl was hot, so she removed her jacket.

This sentence has two clauses and two verbs:

verb 1   verb 2

The girl was hot so she removed her jacket

clause 1   clause 2

In sentences with two clauses, one of the clauses is more important, so it is known as the **main clause**. The main clause can be a sentence on its own. The main clause in this sentence is *The girl was hot*. The main clause is not always the first in a sentence, eg

Although it was snowing, **the match went ahead**.

other clause   main clause

The second, less important clause is known as a **subordinate clause**.

The hotel is in the High Street, which is at the end of Broad Street.

FOCUS

Copy the following sentences. Underline the **main clause** in each one.

1   The hotel is in the High Street, which is at the end of Broad Street.

2   I parked in the wrong place, so my car was towed away.

3   The fruit was rotten when the crowd threw it at the president.

4   I do not wish to know where you have been or how you got home.

5   Because the radiator was leaking, the kitchen was flooded.

6   Although I am old now, I've always enjoyed swimming.

> **HINT**
>
> Subordinate clauses often begin with words like 'who' or 'that'.

INVESTIGATION

Write out the two clauses in each sentence and underline the **main clause**.
The first one has been done for you.

1   Before the house was built the site was just a field.

　　Clause 1 = Before the house was built

　　Clause 2 = <u>the site was just a field</u>.

2   I get on well with people whose star sign is Gemini.
3   The photograph that my mother took was embarrassing.
4   By 12.30, I had only pruned one shrub.
5   People who talk loudly annoy me immensely.
6   My younger sister, who is irritating, takes my CDs.

EXTENSION

Copy the sentences. Add a **main clause** of your own to each of the subordinate clauses. The first one has been done for you.

1   _____ , which was imported from Japan.

　　<u>I have bought a motorcycle</u>, which was imported from Japan.

2   _____ , which was already late.
3   _____ , for which I was grateful.
4   _____ that lives in the next street?
5   _____ that sank in the Atlantic.
6   _____ , which made me suspicious.
7   _____ , who lived next door.
8   _____ , because I had no money.
9   _____ , where the fire had damaged it.
10 _____ , when the figure had disappeared.

MAIN AND SUBORDINATE CLAUSES 2

A **clause** is a group of related words containing a subject and a verb, eg

> *The girl laughed.*

subject   verb

The two most important types of clause are:

- **main clause** (sometimes called an **independent clause**)
- **subordinate clause** (sometimes called a **dependent clause**).

A **simple sentence** is made up of one main clause, which makes sense by itself, eg

> *The boys lived in Richmond.*

A subordinate clause can never stand alone but must accompany a main clause. A subordinate clause does not make sense on its own, eg

> *that my dog likes cheese*

This only makes sense when there is a main clause, eg

> **The vet was surprised** *that my dog likes cheese.*

main clause   subordinate clause

What Long John Silver did with the treasure nobody knows.

FOCUS

Copy the sentences and underline the **main clauses**.

1 What Long John Silver did with the treasure nobody knows.
2 I will take my laptop to Oxford, when I go next week.
3 We don't know what we ought to do next.
4 When the film has finished, we'll go home.
5 My sister, who is very health-conscious, swims regularly to keep fit.
6 While Landee sat indoors watching MTV, Chantal made a herb garden.
7 Wendy wrote books because she knew so much about teaching English.
8 The building that collapsed in the hurricane will cost millions to rebuild.
9 My brother, who is studying at college, never liked sciences at school.

INVESTIGATION

Copy the sentences and underline the **subordinate clauses**.

1. The elderly gentleman, who is 88, lives near his daughter.
2. People who talk too loudly are irritating to others.
3. George Bush, who is President of America, invaded Iraq.
4. Julia, who was standing by the window, called me over to her.
5. Young people who leave school at 16 often regret it later in life.
6. That man who phoned last night said he would call again tomorrow.
7. The photographs that you said you had e-mailed still haven't arrived.
8. Children whose parents smoke often become the victims of passive smoking.

> **HINT**
> Subordinate clauses can also occur in the middle of sentences.

EXTENSION

There are different types of **subordinate** (dependent) **clauses**:

- **Noun clauses** can do anything that nouns can do.
- **Adjectival clauses** give information about a noun or a pronoun and begin with a relative pronoun (*who, whose, whom, which,* and *that*) or a subordinate conjunction (*when* and *where*).
- **Adverbial clauses** tell us something about the sentence's main verb – when, why and under what conditions the action was done.
- **Relative clauses** begin with relative pronouns (*who, whoever, whom, whomever, which* or *that*) or relative adverbs (*when* or *where*).

Copy the sentences. Underline the **subordinate clauses** and say whether they are **adjectival (ADJ)**, **adverbial (ADV)** or **noun clauses (N)**.

1. I don't know what to do when I leave school.
2. Since his wife died, he had been lonely.
3. His brother, who became a mechanic, mended his car for him.
4. Although I broke the window, I did not feel guilty about it.
5. The ship that sank in the tempest went down with all hands.
6. That you fell in love with her so quickly came as a great surprise to us.
7. The whole country was saddened when John Lennon was assassinated.
8. Whatever you end up doing as a career often depends on luck, not just your abilities.

NOUN CLAUSES

One of the main types of subordinate clause is a **noun clause**. Noun clauses act in the same way as nouns.

Certain words show us a noun clause. They are known as **indicators** or **markers**, eg

- *That, if/whether*
- *Wh-*words – *what, when, where, which, who, whom, whose, why* and *how*
- *Wh-ever* words – *whatever, whenever, wherever, whichever, whoever, whomever* and *however*

The choice of the **noun clause marker** depends on the type of clause you are making:

To change a **statement** to a noun clause use *that*, eg

*I know + Manolo refused to learn = I know **that** Manolo refused to learn.*

To change a **yes/no question** to a noun clause, use *if* or *whether*, eg

*Serafina wonders + Does Manolo know how to dive? = Serafina wonders **if** Manolo knows how to dive.*

To change a **wh-question** to a noun clause, use the *wh-*word, eg

*I don't know + Where is Manolo? = I don't know **where** Manolo is.*

I don't know <u>where my mobile phone is.</u>

FOCUS

Copy the sentences and underline the **noun clauses**.

1 I don't know where my mobile phone is.
2 It is a wonder that Manolo learned how to swim.
3 They didn't know if Manolo would dive.
4 The tragedy is that Manolo was arrogant.
5 Manolo didn't listen to what his friends said.
6 Nobody knew what he would do.

INVESTIGATION

Copy the sentences and underline the **noun clauses**.

1 I don't know if you have studied noun clauses before.
2 Your teacher will have decided if you are ready to study noun clauses.
3 I have chosen which noun clauses to teach you.
4 First you will need to know what a noun clause is.
5 I will demonstrate (to you) that you can understand this idea.
6 I mentioned (to you) that other pupils have done well with noun clauses.
7 I promise (you) that the test will be easy and short.
8 Your teacher showed (the class) how to find and write noun clauses.

> **HINT**
> In some examples, the object of the sentence is understood (left out) or assumed. These have been put in brackets for you.

EXTENSION

Copy the sentences. Choose verbs from the list below plus 'that' to fill the blanks, so that the sentences make sense.

advise	ask	command	demand	direct	insist	move
propose	recommend	suggest	urge	agree	answer	
notice	assert	conclude	know	realise	state	think
admit	explain	mention	point out	prove	reply	assure
convince	inform	notify	remind	tell	promise	show

1 Doctors _____ fitness is crucial for health.
2 However, recent research _____ young people do not take enough exercise.
3 The Prime Minister, in a speech to Conference, _____ a campaign to encourage people to exercise.
4 He also _____ better education must begin at primary school.
5 He _____ all young people needed to follow a healthier lifestyle.

ADJECTIVAL CLAUSES

Adjectival clauses are clauses that act as adjectives, providing information about the noun that comes in front of them. Adjectival clauses are introduced by the **relative pronouns** *that*, *who*, *which*, *what*, *whose*, *whom*, *where*, eg

> *Strawberries **that are large and juicy** are the most expensive.*

> adjectival clause

> *My sister, **who is very generous**, lives in Surrey.*

> adjectival clause

Hotels that have many facilities are the most expensive.

FOCUS

Copy the sentences and underline the **adjectival clauses**.

1. Hotels that have many facilities are the most expensive.
2. After eating the scampi, the guests, who had been looking forward to seafood, became unwell.
3. The books that belonged to my sister had been removed.
4. My daughter, whose friend is a model, worries about her.
5. The bicycle, which belonged to my neighbour, was stolen from the garage.
6. The child whom I saw yesterday was eating a huge water-melon.

INVESTIGATION

Copy the sentences. Underline the **adjectival clauses** and circle the **relative pronouns** in the sentences.

1 Those who chose not to come will be disappointed.
2 The books that people read are rarely spiritual.
3 The eggs which they sold were infected with salmonella.
4 The play was a tragedy, which made people cry.
5 They are searching for the child who was reported missing.
6 Did I tell you about the celebrity whom I met?

EXTENSION

There are two kinds of adjectival clauses, restrictive and non-restrictive.

- **Restrictive adjectival clauses** are **dependent adjectival clauses**. They provide essential information for us to understand the meaning of the sentence, eg

   *Strawberries **that are large and juicy** are the most expensive.*

   └─────────────────────┘
   restrictive adjectival clause

This restrictive adjectival clause is limiting the strawberries to the ones that are large and juicy. It is telling us that the most expensive strawberries are large juicy ones, not some other kind of strawberries, so it is essential to the meaning of the sentence.

- **Non-restrictive adjectival clauses** contain additional information that is not essential to identify the subject of the sentence, eg

   *My sister, **who is very generous**, lives in Surrey.*

   └─────────────┘
   non-restrictive adjectival clause

Here, the subject, my sister, is already identified – she lives in Surrey – and the non-restrictive adjectival clause simply provides further information. If we take the non-restrictive adjectival clause away, we still know where my sister lives, and the meaning of the sentence is still clear.

> *HINT*
>
> If there are no commas and you can use 'that', the adjectival clause is restrictive. Non-restrictive adjectival clauses have a comma before and after them.

Copy the sentences and underline the **adjectival clauses**. Say whether they are **restrictive (R)** or **non-restrictive (NR)**.

1 The cat that caught the mouse ate it.
2 All our plans can be completed through programmes that we have developed.
3 The man, whom she despised, killed her cat.
4 The author, who was obsessed with wolves, became a best-seller.
5 The comments, which were made in the letter, led to a court case.
6 The cabinet, which was at the front of the shop window, was an expensive antique.

ADVERBIAL CLAUSES

Adverbial clauses are clauses that act as adverbs, providing information about when, why, where or how something happens, eg

*Tamara, **desperate to finish her coursework**, stayed up until 1 a.m.*

adverbial clause

Question: Why did Tamara stay up until 1 a.m.?
Answer: She was desperate to finish her coursework.

So, this adverbial clause tells us **why** something happened. Adverbial clauses provide additional information about the main events of a sentence and often include a verb ending in *-ed* or *-ing*, eg

*Feel**ing** frustrated, Landee withdrew from the course.*

adverbial clause

An adverbial clause is dependent on an accompanying independent clause. Adverbial clauses can come in three positions:

- **before** the independent clause, when they are divided from the independent clause by a comma, eg

  When the supermodel entered the room, *he reacted appreciatively.*

  adverbial clause

- in the **middle** of a sentence, when they are enclosed by commas, eg

  *My sister, **determined to become a magistrate,** is taking a course in law.*

  adverbial clause

- **after** the independent clause, when they are not separated from the independent clause by any punctuation, eg

  *Beth and Josh were attracted to each other **as they chatted**.*

  adverbial clause

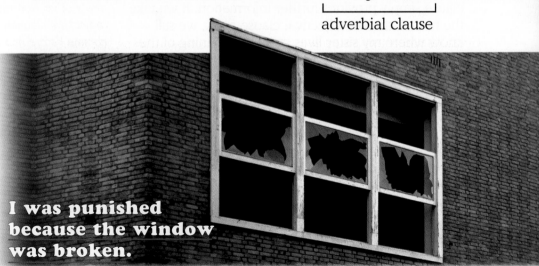

I was punished because the window was broken.

FOCUS

Copy the sentences and underline the **adverbial clauses**.

1 I was punished because the window was broken.
2 Before my bedroom was decorated, it looked depressing.
3 Agatha made toast and tea as I boiled the eggs.
4 We had to move house before we were really ready.
5 The whole school was saddened when Mr Hicks left.
6 Although Buffy broke the window, Spike took the blame for it.

INVESTIGATION

Adverbial clauses usually begin with a word known as an **adverbial subordinator** or **subordinating conjunction**, eg

| when | if | because | as | while |
| after | before | until | since |

Copy the sentences. Underline the **adverbial clauses** and circle the **adverbial subordinator** or **subordinating conjunction**.

1 I saw the film *Lathe of Heaven* before I left for Australia.
2 Wherever there are computers, there are computer viruses.
3 Since Father died, we have lost many details of our family history.
4 After the crops are harvested, they are sold to the supermarkets.
5 Since the boy was disruptive, he was transferred to another school.
6 I didn't telephone Amindra because I am frightened she'll reject me.
7 If we don't stop burning fossil fuels, global warming will disrupt our climate.
8 She took a herbalist's course so that she could set up her own business.

EXTENSION

Copy the sentences. Underline the **adverbial clause** and circle the **main independent clause** that it accompanies.

1 I haven't been swimming since we all went last month.
2 Neal cycles where there is a great deal of traffic.
3 He sat there as if you would have to bulldoze him to get him to move.
4 She writes letters because she feels obliged to do so.
5 I will write you a reference letter if you give me a copy of your CV.
6 Since we all went to Dartmoor last year, I haven't been hill walking.
7 Because she enjoys it, she plays the piano.
8 If you will provide me with a copy of your will, I will witness it for you.

RELATIVE CLAUSES

A **relative clause** provides more details about a noun or pronoun, giving essential information to identify or clarify the person or thing we are talking about.

- **Relative pronouns** are the small words that join relative clauses:

    for things, we use 'which' or 'that'
    for places, 'where'
    for people, 'who'
    for time, 'when'.

Relative clauses can either be **restrictive** or **non-restrictive**.

- **Restrictive relative clauses** give us essential information in order to complete the meaning of the main clause, eg

    Where is the pupil **who is going to the theatre**?

    main clause   relative pronoun   restrictive relative clause

The relative clause here tells us that the pupil we are looking for is the one going to the theatre, and not any other pupil, so it is restrictive.

- **Non-restrictive relative clauses** add information to the main clause, but are not needed for the meaning to be clear. Non-restrictive relative clauses have commas at the beginning and the end, eg

    The Freelander, **which is my preferred choice,** *has four-wheel drive.*

    non-restrictive relative clause

There's the singer who went to school with my sister.

FOCUS

Copy the sentences. Complete them using the **relative pronouns** *which/who/when/where/whose/that*.

1 There's the singer _____ went to school with my sister.
2 I know an inn _____ sells real ale.
3 Do you know a shop _____ I can buy a camcorder?
4 Leonardo da Vinci, ____ painted the *Mona Lisa*, died in the early 16th century.
5 The language _____ people speak in Ireland is called Irish Gaelic.
6 This is Bob, _____ works in the adventure playground at Deptford.
7 I need to speak to the person _____ deals with national insurance contributions.
8 I hate it _____ my daughters ask me to go through their essays.

INVESTIGATION

Copy the sentences and underline the **relative clauses**. Say whether they are **restrictive (R)** or **non-restrictive (NR)** relative clauses.

1 The band, which is playing tonight, is my favourite.
2 This is the painting that I like best.
3 Is he the lawyer who is going to represent the burglar?
4 That girl, who is going to the Summer Ball, drove an expensive sports car.
5 The guitarist, whose hand was injured, received enormous compensation.
6 Doctor Anneka, whom I was hoping to see, wasn't on duty.

EXTENSION

Copy the sentences and put in the correct **relative pronoun**.

1 What's the name of the boy which/who phoned you yesterday?
2 The thing that/who I can't understand is why he wouldn't tell anyone about his first wife.
3 The face, that/which a few moments ago had been pleasant and smiling, now seemed bitter and resentful.
4 The woman which/whom he married was mentally unstable.
5 I can remember a teacher whose/whom hair grew nearly to her waist.
6 Her father, that/whom I never met, was an alcoholic.
7 We used to go on holiday to France where/which you could really relax and forget your troubles.
8 One of the women whom/which I admire most is Louise Brooks.

PUNCTUATION OF QUOTED (DIRECT) SPEECH

Quotation marks (or **speech marks**) ("...") show us when somebody is talking. All the words that are actually spoken and their punctuation are placed inside speech marks.

- When the direct speech comes before the person speaking, a comma is placed in front of the second (closing) speech mark, eg

  "Come here. I want to give you something," said Davina.

- When the direct speech comes after the person speaking, the comma comes before the first (opening) speech mark, eg

  Davina said, "Come here. I want to give you something."

  Here, the actual speech has two sentences so both sentences start with a capital letter.

- When the person speaking comes in between two sentences of direct speech, a comma is used before the closing speech mark of the first sentence, and a full stop is placed before the opening speech mark for the second speech, eg

  "Come here," said Davina. "I want to give you something."

- When the person speaking comes in between two parts of the same sentence of direct speech, then we use a comma before the closing speech mark of the first speech, and another comma before the start of the second speech, eg

  "If you were to come here," said Davina, "you would see something interesting."

  She is still speaking the same sentence, so *you* does not start with a capital letter.

- Start a new paragraph every time the speaker changes.

"Stop!" shouted the security guard.

FOCUS

Copy these sentences and put the **speech marks** in the correct places.

1 Stop! shouted the security guard.
2 What time is it? asked Clare.
3 Hello, said the stranger.
4 What are you doing? said Aisling.
5 Wait a minute, said George. Don't I know you from somewhere?
6 I know, said Beth. We'll go to Pizza Express.

INVESTIGATION

Copy these sentences and put the **speech marks** in the correct places.

1 Quick! Pass to me! shouted Beckham. I'm not being marked.
2 Can I help you? asked the shop assistant. You look a bit lost.
3 Oh no! Don't let Forlan take the penalty! shouted Neville.
4 I'll meet you in town, said Naomi. Just outside Waterstones.
5 I've mislaid my keys, said Grace. They must be here somewhere.
6 Look at that painting, said Jane Russell. It's wonderful!

EXTENSION

Copy the passage and add the **speech marks**.

I'm afraid I have some bad news, Mr McPartland said to
Mrs Reilly. Your son has had an accident. What's happened?
Mrs Reilly asked. Is it serious? Will he have to go to hospital?
Will he have to have an operation? Mr Reilly asked. Now don't
worry, Mr McPartland replied. It's not as bad as all that. He's
had a fall and he may have broken his arm. How did that happen?
Mr Reilly exclaimed. I suppose he's a bit shocked, said Mrs Reilly.
He's a little bit shaken up, Mr McPartland said.

HINT

Remember to start a
new paragraph each time
the speaker changes.

REPORTED (INDIRECT) SPEECH

Where direct speech quotes exactly what is said, **reported (indirect) speech** reports a conversation after it has happened, eg

Quoted (direct) speech: *"I don't like cats," Julie said.*
Reported (indirect) speech: *Julie said that she doesn't like cats.*

Reported (indirect) speech differs from quoted (direct) speech in the following ways:

1 Quoted speech has quotation marks; reported speech does **not** use quotation marks.

2 In reported speech the pronoun often changes. In the example above, the pronoun *I* is used in the quoted speech, whereas the sentence with reported speech uses the pronoun *she*.

3 In reported speech, the word *that* is often used after *said*.

4 Quoted speech is exactly what the person said. Reported speech is **not** exactly what the person said, so you can change some words to make the sentence appropriate and logical.

5 The verb in reported speech is changed to the past tense.

Reporting verbs

The most common **reporting verbs** are *said*, *told* and *asked*.
We use:

• *asked* to report questions, eg We **asked** where the station was.

• *told* with an object, eg Simon **told** Alice to go to St Martin's.

• *said that* without an object, eg I **said that** I didn't want to go home.

• *said to* with an object, eg She **said** it **to** herself.

Many other verbs may be used as reporting verbs, eg

agree	yell	beg	promise
reply	boast	advise	remind
report	accuse	deny	tell
scream	complain	order	warn
shout	apologise	suggest	say

Tim said he'd played golf. R

FOCUS

Copy the sentences and say whether they are **quoted speech** (**Q**) or **reported speech** (**R**).

1 Tim said he'd played golf.
2 "I've finished my revision."
3 Nancy asked me why I'd left the party.
4 "It will snow tomorrow."
5 He asked me if I wanted to go to see the film.
6 Chris said, "I like photography and computers."

INVESTIGATION

Copy and change the following sentences from **quoted speech** to **reported speech**.

1 "I am watching TV," Lydia said, "so you can't watch a DVD."
2 Doctor Golby said, "I worked all day!"
3 Mr Berlacone said, "I will be visiting Italy in December."
4 The weather forecaster stated, "It may rain today."
5 The journalist yelled, "I have to go to the airport, now!"
6 Then Dad said, "I must meet your mother in town."

EXTENSION

Copy and change the following sentences from **reported speech** to **quoted speech**.

1 The policeman said that I should calm down.
2 I responded that I needed to leave the room.
3 David said he loved visiting China.
4 Martin said that he could be a great teacher.
5 Sunil told me to close the doors.
6 Jasmin will always say that she has already done her coursework.

SENTENCE TYPES

Sentences:

- start with a capital letter A, B, C, ...
- end with a full stop (.), exclamation mark (!) or question mark (?)
- contain at least one clause, with a subject and a verb

There are four types of sentences:

- **Statements (declarative sentences)** state facts or ideas and end with a full stop, eg

  School starts on 4 September.

- **Questions (interrogative sentences)** ask questions and finish with a question mark, eg

  Are you buying a motorbike?

- **Imperative sentences** give orders or make requests. A request ends with a full stop but a command or order ends with an exclamation mark, eg

  Please close the garage door. (request)
  Tidy your room, now! (order)

- **Exclamatory sentences** express strong feelings and end with an exclamation mark, eg

  I hate meat!

Birds fly south in winter.   S

FOCUS

Copy these sentences and identify whether they are **statements (S)**, **questions (Q)**, **imperatives (I)** or **exclamations (E)**.

1 Birds fly south in winter.
2 Why aren't you coming out tonight?
3 Do all trees lose their leaves in the autumn?
4 Don't do that.
5 Oh, good grief!
6 What kind of an answer was that?
7 Damn!
8 I enjoy music a great deal.
9 Bring me your book.

INVESTIGATION

Copy the sentences and identify each type – **statement (S)**, **question (Q)**, **imperative (I)** or **exclamation (E)**. Put the correct punctuation at the end of the sentence.

1 What is the time
2 It was hot yesterday
3 What a beautiful baby
4 Use 100 grams of flour
5 Do not walk on the grass
6 I think it is going to rain today
7 Are you going clubbing tonight

EXTENSION

Some sentences may not fit neatly into a particular category.
We sometimes use **rhetorical questions**, for which we do not expect an answer, eg

What do you expect me to do about it?

A **question** can also be an **exclamation**, expressing strong feelings, eg

Wasn't that film brilliant?

Copy the table below and complete it with eight sentences of your own.
Use two **statements**, two **questions**, two **imperatives** and two **exclamations**.

Statements	Questions	Imperatives	Exclamations
1 _____	1 _____	1 _____	1 _____
2 _____	2 _____	2 _____	2 _____

SUBJECT AND PREDICATE

Every complete sentence contains two parts: a **subject** and a **predicate**.

Subject

The subject is the person, place, or thing that acts, is acted on, or is described in the sentence.

- The **simple subject** answers the questions: Who? What? The subject is who, or what the sentence is about, eg

  Charlie painted.

- The **complete subject** is the simple subject and the words connected to it, eg

  Artistic Charlie painted.

- A **compound subject** is two or more subjects joined by a conjunction, eg

  Charlie and Neal live in Camden.

Predicate

The predicate is the action or description that tells us something about the subject, eg

  The girl skipped.

  subject   predicate

- A **simple predicate** is a complete verb (a verb and any helping verbs), eg

  *She **was dancing**.*

- A **complete predicate** is a simple predicate and all its extra information, eg

  *She **sang quietly**.*

- A **compound predicate** is two or more predicates with a single subject, eg

  *She **stayed awake** and **danced all night**.*

The dog is barking.

FOCUS

Copy the sentences. Underline the **subject** and circle the **predicate**.

1 The dog is barking.
2 Chloe is funny.
3 Gillian drives fast.
4 Felicity is flirtatious.
5 Ali is rich and romantic.
6 Harry drew a picture.

INVESTIGATION

Copy the sentences and underline the **simple subject** in each one.

1 The ignition starts the car.
2 An arrow on the sign indicates the direction.
3 The keys on the key-ring didn't open the door.
4 The student typed the essay on the laptop.
5 Words appear like magic on the screen.
6 Ian's friend from school wants to work in computers.
7 The teacher uses the interactive whiteboard for teaching.
8 Some students experience difficulties with mis-spelled words.
9 Some students play games on the computer.
10 The computer in my study can speak my text.
11 Sonia dreams of having a computer of her own.
12 My sister uses e-mail to contact me.

EXTENSION

Copy the sentences and fill in the gaps. Say whether you have used a **subject** or **predicate**.

1 The sailor _____ .
2 _____ is on the ground floor.
3 _____ has never been repaired.
4 The old church _____ .
5 _____ is staying in a chalet.
6 The new estate _____ .
7 _____ hid in a shack in the mountains.
8 _____ was wrecked on a rocky reef.

DIRECT AND INDIRECT OBJECT

A **direct object** is the word or words (noun or pronoun) in a sentence showing the person or thing receiving the action of the verb, eg

> The girl broke **the window**.

The window is the direct object of the verb that comes before it. It tells us who or what received the action of the verb *broke*.

An **indirect object** comes before the direct object. It tells us to whom or for whom the action of the verb is being done, eg

> She told **him** her **opinion**.

    indirect object   direct object

In this sentence, *opinion* is the direct object but *him* is an indirect object, explaining to whom the direct object is directed. Indirect objects must be nouns or pronouns and answer the question *to*, *for* or *upon whom* or *what* the verb is acting, eg

> She sent letters to Heather and Sonia.

Letters is the direct object of the verb *sent*. Heather and Sonia are receiving those letters, so we say that Heather and Sonia are indirect objects.

Pass me that towel.

FOCUS

Copy the sentences. Underline the **direct objects**. Circle the **indirect objects**. Not all sentences contain indirect objects.

1. Pass me that towel.
2. Play me a tune.
3. The captain picked the team.
4. He fed the dog cheese.
5. I'll give her a piece of my mind.
6. The champion lifted the weights.
7. The vision of the monster terrified George.
8. Auntie May sent Jackie a parcel.

INVESTIGATION

Copy the sentences. Underline the **direct objects** and circle the **indirect objects**. Not all sentences contain indirect objects.

1. Felix put lights on his bicycle.
2. A huge fireball devastated Dresden.
3. Researchers have studied cancer.
4. The girl telephoned Clarence.
5. Amazon sent the parcel to me.
6. The nurse gave the visitor tea.
7. She sent Jim a present.
8. The pupil gave the teacher his pen.

> **HINT**
>
> An indirect object is the noun or pronoun that comes between an action verb and its direct object.

EXTENSION

Copy the sentences. Complete them by adding either a **direct** or an **indirect object**.

1. Ellie likes _____.
2. Call _____!
3. Mary sent _____.
4. The pupil completed _____.
5. I'm injured! Get _____ a doctor!
6. I wouldn't give _____ the time of day.
7. The rev counter gives _____ a way of knowing the speed of the car's engine.
8. The Princess told her butler many _____.

SUBJECT–VERB AGREEMENT

A sentence has a **subject** and a **verb**. The subject noun and the verb must go together; this is called **subject–verb agreement**.

Singular subjects must have **singular verbs**, eg

She reads many books at school.

singular subject   singular verb

Plural subjects need **plural verbs**, eg

They carry many books at school.

plural subject   plural verb

A **collective noun** is the name given to a single group of things, eg

A single *herd* of cattle

A single *flock* of sheep

Collective nouns are always followed by singular verbs, eg

The flock of flamingoes flutters like pink flames.

singular subject   singular verb

Prices of goods and common food are singular, eg

That magazine is a high price.

singular subject   singular verb

The badger ambles along the hedgerow.

FOCUS

Copy the sentences. Choose and underline the **singular** or the **plural verb** to match the **subject** in each sentence.

1 The badger amble/ambles along the hedgerow.
2 Burglars steals/steal from other people's houses.
3 They is/are careless about locking their doors.
4 The local football team play/plays on Sundays.
5 Fish and chips is/are my favourite meal.
6 Each passport has/have a photograph in it.

INVESTIGATION

Copy the sentences and underline the **subject** of the verb.
Circle the **verb**.

1 Three-quarters of the wheat is spoiled.
2 There are several explanations for the outbreak of World War 2.
3 Neither the headteacher nor the teachers are to blame.
4 Neither of these alternatives is very appealing.
5 Some of the pupils in the dining hall have finished already.
6 Has either the Prime Minister or his office contacted you?
7 None of the MPs has stated how they will vote on the issue.
8 The examiner raised the candidate's grade as a result of a re-mark.

> ## HINT
> In formal writing, when 'either' and 'neither' appear as a subject alone, ie without 'or' and 'nor', they are singular, even if the subject seems to be two things.

EXTENSION

Copy the sentences and underline the **subject** of the verb.
Circle the **verb**.

1 Either the organisers or the headteacher have to be responsible for the community concert.
2 The majority of the pupils is opposed to the war with Iraq.
3 If the leadership group takes this attitude, there is little hope of a compromise.
4 Half of the pupils did not revise properly for their exams this year.
5 Of the voting so far, half favours abolishing school uniform.
6 Some of the straw stored in the barn, as well as some pieces of equipment, was destroyed in the fire.
7 Either is fine as far as I am concerned.
8 The budget presented by the government, together with some other laws, is going to result in higher taxes.

CHECK-UP 1

Main (independent) clauses

Copy each sentence and say whether the clauses in italics are **main (independent) clauses** or not.

1 The forest fire began *because a camper was irresponsible*.
2 The doctor *who bought my house* is moving in next month.
3 *Wherever Maggie goes* I have to keep track of her.
4 According to Mrs Etherington, the Head of Maths, *the binary system is part of the syllabus*.
5 Did you know *that Royal Holloway is a London University college*?
6 Mr Keats will buy the bookshop *if the bank gives him a mortgage*.
7 *She won the competition* because she had practised for hours every week.
8 *Whatever you decide* won't upset me.
9 *I saw the job advertised in the local paper* and applied for it.
10 *I was impressed that* you were so sportsmanlike.

Subordinate (dependent) clauses

Copy each sentence and underline the **subordinate (dependent) clauses**.

1 While scratching its fleas, the dog toppled over backwards.
2 Alan Rickman is Charlie's favourite actor but I like Hugh Grant.
3 Before the concert began, the lead guitarist bent down to unplug his guitar; this simple movement set off a chain reaction of unfortunate events.
4 When the mink approached, the Canada goose took off.
5 Mum always wanted to live in Richmond but Dad wanted to live in Ireland.
6 While cutting the grass, I heard a noisy microlight flying overhead.
7 Joanne had worked hard for straight A grades in her exams, and when the results were displayed, she discovered her efforts had been rewarded.
8 Bert carefully lined up the pieces on the draughts board; however, Peggy's elbow caught the edge of the board, and both board and pieces flew on to the floor.

Clauses

A Use the words in brackets to copy and complete the sentences with **subordinate noun clauses**, starting with *that*. Be sure to include *that* and use appropriate verb tenses.

1 It seems ___. (my favourite band / just / issue / a new CD)
2 We are convinced ___. (the murderer / be arrested)
3 Amy did not realise _____. (she / forget / to pay / for the scarf)
4 I was pleasantly surprised _____. (the stars of the film / not get married / in the end)

B Copy the sentences. Take the question in brackets and use it to make a **noun clause**. Then put the noun clause in the blank, starting with *if* or *whether*.

1 (Did the singer get help writing his Number One hit?) We wonder _____.

2 (Has Terry Pratchett agreed to do a book signing in Taunton?)
Do you know _____?

3 (Should she write her autobiography?) She is considering _____.

4 (Does your boyfriend like fantasy literature?) I'm not sure _____.

5 (Do soaps have educational value?) The question is _____.

C Copy and complete the sentences by adding an **adjectival clause**.

1 This is the city _____.

2 The Headteacher whom _____ just resigned.

3 Do you know the man _____?

4 The magazine article _____ is not very informative.

5 Here is an artist _____.

Reported (indirect) speech

Copy the sentences. Change the quoted (direct) speech in each pair of sentences into **reported (indirect) speech**, by putting the verbs into the correct tenses and changing the pronouns.

1 "I teach English at Court Fields School."

He said that _____ English at Court
Fields School.

2 "I am training to become a potter."

She said that _____ to become a potter.

3 "I am not going to give up yet."

He said that _____ yet.

4 "I have to get a scholarship to go to Oxford."

She said that _____ a scholarship to go to Oxford.

5 "I might have to get a part-time job while I'm studying."

He said that _____ a part-time job
while _____ studying.

SIMPLE SENTENCES

A **subject** and **predicate**, together, form a **simple sentence**. 'Simple' refers to the basic structure of a sentence, not whether the ideas are simple or complicated. The basic construction of the sentence is simple, eg

Tammy   likes pasta.

   subject   predicate

The girl from Devon with the 'cool' clothes prefers pasta.

   subject   predicate

These are simple sentences because both consist of a subject and a predicate. They both mean *She likes pasta*. Both sentences have the same structure.

Taking their shoes off   No

FOCUS

Copy the sentences. After each, write *Yes* for the examples that are complete, **simple sentences**. Write *No* for examples that are not proper, simple sentences.

1 Taking their shoes off
2 Bothered by anything
3 I knew it
4 CD without any tracks
5 Happily dancing in the street
6 She found the lost pencil-case

INVESTIGATION

Copy the sentences. Circle each **subject** and underline each **predicate.**

1 Lewis is a boy.
2 He loves food.
3 What he likes to eat is banana.
4 Lewis and Henry have banana sandwiches.
5 Banana sandwiches are not provided at playgroup.
6 Little children can be rough in their play.
7 Nappies are a nuisance.
8 Babies' buggies are expensive if you buy the latest models.
9 Babies are smelly and noisy.
10 Babies are fascinating to watch.

EXTENSION

Copy the sentences. Fill the gaps by putting in either a **subject** or a **main verb** of your own.

1 Greg _____ to prison.
2 School _____ is important.
3 Jonathan _____ asleep.
4 _____ is within your talents.
5 He _____ about Rivendell.
6 The _____ are coloured yellow.
7 _____ went to Wimbledon College.
8 _____ is a town famous for tennis.
9 Maggie _____ every detail of the sculpture.
10 I _____ the Yanomamo tribe from the Amazon.

COMPOUND SENTENCES

To express more complicated ideas, it is sometimes necessary to join simple sentences together. When we join simple sentences together, we make **compound sentences**. There are three basic ways of combining simple sentences into compound sentences.

1 Use a **semi-colon by itself** to join two closely-related simple sentences, eg

> *Some writers influenced Shakespeare. More writers were influenced by him.*

becomes

> *Some writers influenced Shakespeare; more writers were influenced by him.*

2 Use a **semi-colon and a conjunctive adverb, followed by a comma**, eg

> *Many admire Stanley Kubrick's films. Some don't understand his work.*

becomes

> *Many admire Stanley Kubrick's films; **however**, some don't understand his work.*

3 Use a **comma and a coordinating conjunction**, eg

> *Ben Jonson wrote superb essays. Scholars read them.*

becomes

> *Ben Jonson wrote superb essays, **and** scholars read them.*

Rugby is a tough game; however, many people enjoy its tactical challenges.

FOCUS

Copy and join these pairs of simple sentences into **compound sentences**.
Use each of the three ways opposite, at least once.

1 Rugby is a tough game. Many people enjoy its tactical challenges.
2 Some pupils work very hard. Other pupils are unmotivated.
3 Holly went to the library to revise. Ivy went to the pool.
4 The pupil was exhausted. She fell asleep in the classroom.
5 We were late for our flight. Snow had caused a traffic jam.
6 Imran could not find his turban. He could not find his shoes.

INVESTIGATION

Copy and complete these **compound sentences**, following the instructions
given in the brackets to fill in the gaps.

1 My daughter likes berries _____ I like citrus fruits.
   (comma and coordinating conjunction)
2 Citrus fruits are often sharp and refreshing _____ they are ideal
   in tropical climates.
   (semi-colon with a conjunctive adverb)
3 Food rots quickly in hot countries _____ spoiled fruits are
   sometimes used in cooking.
   (comma with coordinating conjunction)
4 Bread and cakes are made from over-ripe fruit _____ there are
   many recipes for fruit bread and cake.
   (semi-colon by itself)
5 Do they want to stay here _____ will they come with us?
   (comma and coordinating conjunction)

EXTENSION

Copy the sentences. Explain how each sentence qualifies as
a **compound sentence**.

1 Neither they will go, nor will I.
   This sentence qualifies as a compound sentence because _____
2 I collected her on time, but she still missed her train.
   This sentence qualifies as a compound sentence because _____
3 She had finished the book, or so the teacher assumed.
   This sentence qualifies as a compound sentence because _____
4 Beth understands Anglo-Saxon; she studied it at Cambridge.
   This sentence qualifies as a compound sentence because _____
5 I was delighted to see my ex-pupils again; I haven't seen them for ages.
   This sentence qualifies as a compound sentence because _____

COMPLEX SENTENCES

Complex sentences consist of one main (independent) clause and one or more subordinate (dependent) clauses. **Complex sentences** make one idea depend on (subordinate to) another, where:

- the clauses are connected by a **time** sequence, eg

  *John Reilly was promoted to the rank of captain **before** the end of World War 2.*

- one clause expresses **cause** and the other clause explains the **effect**, eg

  *The major **was killed** in Burma by **stepping on a Japanese mine**.*

  effect   cause

- one clause expresses the **conditions** necessary for the other clause to have effect, eg

  *Captain Reilly was promoted to major **in order to provide a commanding officer**.*

Because a complex sentence makes one clause depend on another, it always has a **subordinator** (*because, since, after, although,* or *when*) or a **relative pronoun** (*that, who,* or *which*).

She was distressed when her son was jailed.

FOCUS

Copy the **complex sentences**, underlining the **subject** of the main clause, circling the **main verb**, and highlighting the **subordinators** and **relative pronouns**.

1 She was distressed when her son was jailed.
2 When José handed in his essay, he forgot to give in the last page.
3 The teacher returned the essay once she noticed the error.
4 The pupils who are successful are working hard.
5 After they finished their research, José and Consuela went to the dining hall.
6 José and Consuela went home after they finished dinner.

INVESTIGATION

Subordinate (dependent) clauses can act as nouns, adjectives or adverbs within a sentence or another clause. The most common function of noun clauses is as direct or indirect objects.

Copy the sentences and underline the **subordinate clauses**. Say whether they are acting as nouns, adjectives, adverbs, or as objects.

1 I said that I wanted to go out.
2 The man who burgled the house is now in jail.
3 That he was wrong was hard for him to admit.
4 The players cried because their team lost the Final.
5 Tony gave whoever wanted one a copy of his story.
6 After they won the cup, the players had a celebration.

EXTENSION

Copy the sentences and complete them by adding **main** or **subordinate clauses** of your own.

1 _____ that was a good idea.
2 The customer complained _____.
3 He remembered _____.
4 _____ that Brad Pitt gave Jennifer Aniston.
5 The pupils weren't listening _____.

NEGATIVES AND DOUBLE NEGATIVES

These words are known as **negative** words:

no   not   none   nothing   nowhere   neither

nobody   no one   hardly   scarcely   barely

Words combined with *-n't* and the word *not* are also negative words.

When you use negative words only **once** in a sentence, your sentence will be negative, eg

*I do **not** want anything. = I want nothing.*

negative used only once (negative sentence)

If you use negative words **twice** in one sentence, the sentence becomes positive instead of negative. Two negatives in the same sentence cancel each other out and create a positive sentence, eg

*It is **not** an **un**common sight. = It is a common sight.*

negative used twice (positive sentence)

Katie did _not_ want Neal to leave.

FOCUS

Copy the sentences and underline the **negative words**.

1   Katie did not want Neal to leave.
2   You have no idea what I'm saying!
3   He runs strongly, but not very stylishly.
4   No pupils from the secondary school gained high grades in their GCSE exams.
5   There weren't any chickens left alive when the fox got into the hen-house.
6   I've got no time to waste, today.
7   I haven't any time for games.

INVESTIGATION

Copy the sentences. Choose the word from the brackets that makes
each sentence **negative** without making it a double negative. The first
one has been done for you.

1   The survivors in the life-boat had not had ____ water for days. (any/no)

   The survivors in the life-boat had not had any water for days.

2   I shouldn't have said _____ about your girlfriend. (anything, nothing)

3   By the end of the film, I _____ hardly stand the tension. (could, couldn't)

4   Why _____ I bring only one suitcase? (can, can't)

5   The keys _____ nowhere to be found. (were, weren't)

6   Tim is a diabetic and won't eat _____ of those sweets. (any, none)

7   The pupils didn't say _____ about the exam. (nothing, anything)

8   United don't need _____ one additional defender. (but, more than)

9   They can't _____ hope to become rich. (ever, never)

10 By the afternoon, there _____ barely a flake of snow left. (was, wasn't)

11 I have hardly _____ seen a more beautiful girl. (ever, never)

EXTENSION

On a separate sheet of paper, write sentences of your own, using each of
the **negative words** correctly. The first one has been done for you.

1   (barely) *I <u>barely</u> got my fingers out of the machine in time.*

2   (but) _____

3   (hardly) _____

4   (never) _____

5   (nowhere) _____

6   (shouldn't) _____

7   (cannot) _____

8   (wouldn't) _____

9   (could not) _____

10 (shall not) _____

ACTIVE AND PASSIVE VOICE

Sentences can be in the **active** or **passive voice**. The voice of a verb has to do with whether or not the subject of a sentence acts upon something else, or whether the subject is acted upon. In the active voice, the subject does the action (verb) to something (object); in the passive voice, the subject is acted upon, eg

> **Active voice**: *The toddler left a trail of destruction.*
> **Passive voice**: *A trail of destruction was left by the toddler.*

The active voice is a clearer and more powerful form of writing, using fewer words to convey the same meaning, eg

> **Active voice**: *Molly ate the nectarines.*
> subject action object

> **Passive voice**: *The nectarines were eaten by Molly.*
> subject verb

Passive voice is quite easy to find:

1 Find any form of the verb *to be* – *is, was, were, will be, would be*, etc.

2 Is the verb *to be* followed by a verb in the past tense, eg
   looked, chased, thought?

3 Does the word *by* appear after the whole verb? If it does it may indicate the passive voice, though the word *by* does not have to appear in the sentence in order for the verb to be passive.

The gate had been left open. P

FOCUS

Copy the sentences. Underline the **subject** of the sentence. Say whether the sentence is in the **active voice** (**A**) or the **passive voice** (**P**).

1 The gate had been left open.
2 The boy hit his sister.
3 The sister was hit by her brother.
4 The ball broke the window.
5 The ball was punctured by the dog's teeth.
6 The dog had escaped from the garden.

INVESTIGATION

These sentences are written in the **passive voice**. Rewrite them in the **active voice**.

1 The story was written by my brother-in-law.
2 Anyone in distress is helped by Simon.
3 Patients will be made well by this treatment!
4 Many inventions were designed by Leonardo da Vinci.
5 This beautiful room was created by your friends?
6 Many historical sites are excavated by dedicated archaeologists.
7 Melissa was chosen by James to be his partner.
8 Charles was enraged by Ned's critical comments.

EXTENSION

On a separate sheet of paper, write four pairs of sentences. The first sentence in each pair should be in the **active voice** and the second sentence should put the first into the **passive voice**. The first one has been done for you.

1 a) Julia rode my bicycle into the pond.
   b) My bicycle was ridden into the pond by Julia.

2 a) _____
   b) _____
3 a) _____
   b) _____
4 a) _____
   b) _____
5 a) _____
   b) _____

SENTENCE VARIETY 1

To make writing more interesting and effective, sentences need to be **varied**. Sentences can be joined or restructured in many different ways.

If your sentences are short and clumsy, you can make them more varied by:

- using **coordinating conjunctions** to join complete sentences, clauses, and phrases, eg

  Women are from Venus. Men are from Mars.

  becomes

  *Women are from Venus **and** men are from Mars.*

- linking and prioritising ideas so that one sentence carries the main idea and the other related sentence is changed to a **subordinate clause** in a longer sentence, eg

  Traffic is increasing. Few people want to share cars.

  *Traffic is increasing **as few people want to share cars**.*

  └──────────┘ └────────────────────────┘
      main idea   subordinate clause

- sometimes putting the **subordinate clause** first in the sentence, eg

  The UK has been too dependent on foreign oil. Sustainable energy is now being investigated.

  subordinate clause

  Although the UK has been too dependent on foreign oil, *sustainable energy is now being investigated.*

  └────────────────────────────────────┘
                 main clause

He had teeth like the stars and they came out at night.

FOCUS

Copy the pairs of sentences and join them using **coordinating conjunctions**.

HINT
Remember FANBOYS for the coordinating conjunctions: For, And, Nor, But, Or, Yet, So

1 He had teeth like the stars. They came out at night.
2 The school needed a sports hall. The budget was inadequate.
3 He overslept yesterday. He was late for his exam.
4 Stella grabbed Peter by the hair. He quickly agreed to do what she said.
5 Ian caught a rainbow trout. Veronica caught flu.
6 Justine married Richard Casey. She became Justine Casey.

INVESTIGATION

Copy the sentences. Add a **main (independent) clause** or **subordinate (dependent) clauses** to complete and give variety to each of them.

1 I will be a guest at the Awards Evening provided _____.
2 Ray, _____ , has decided to continue working.
3 With no plan in mind, _____.
4 _____, she will be able to drive to the beach with her friends.
5 Now that Heather has graduated, _____.

EXTENSION

On a separate sheet of paper, write five sentences of your own that contain one **main (independent) clause** and at least one **subordinate (dependent) clause**. Use some of the following **indicator words** to show the dependent clause:

after   although   as   as if   because   before   even if
even though   if   if only   rather than   since   that   though
unless   until   when   where   whereas   wherever   whether
which   while

1 _____
2 _____
3 _____
4 _____
5 _____

SENTENCE VARIETY 2

If the subject or topic is repeated in a series of sentences, look at ways of improving the **variety** of the sentences by:

- putting one sentence inside another using a **relative clause** starting with one of the **relative pronouns** *which, who, whom, that,* eg

  The bell, **which is rung on Sunday mornings***, calls people to church.*

- cutting out *be* verbs (*is, was, were, are*) and using a **present** or **past participle** instead.

  Present participles end in *-ing* (*listening, weaving, thinking*), eg

  Listening *at the door, she heard their gossip.*

  Past participles usually end in *-ed, -en, -d, -n,* or *-t,* (*beaten, raved, dealt, fought*), eg

  Beaten*, the enemy retreated in panic.*

- turning a clause into a **prepositional phrase** (a phrase beginning with a preposition), using prepositions such as *above, across, against, beneath, beside, between, despite, during, except, until,* eg

  The sword **beside the crusader's grave** *was broken and bloody.*

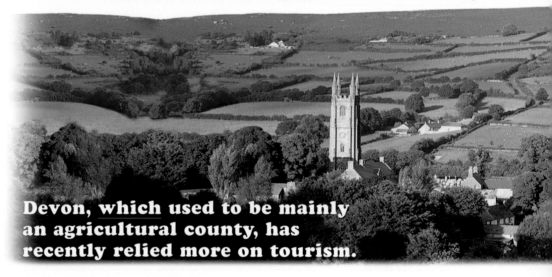

Devon, which used to be mainly an agricultural county, has recently relied more on tourism.

FOCUS

Copy each pair of sentences. Put the less important sentence inside the main point as a **relative clause** and underline the relative pronoun.

1 Devon used to be mainly an agricultural county. It has recently relied more on tourism.

2 One of the cameras was not packed very well. It was damaged during the flight.

3 The holiday was cancelled because James was ill. It was booked for June.

4 Doctor Sherlock practises medicine in Devon. She helped my friend recover from a farm accident.

INVESTIGATION

Rewrite and improve the variety of the sentences by moving the clauses in italics with the underlined **participles** to a different position in each sentence.

1. The towns of Ilfracombe, Woolacombe and Braunton are <u>situated</u> *along the north coast of Devon*.

2. Chris, *<u>sitting</u> at the back of the class <u>engaged</u> in conversation*, disrupted the lesson.

3. Jo Bloggs, *<u>having been</u> a professional rugby player*, was a good choice to coach the local rugby team.

4. The puppy, *<u>running</u> happily across the fields to its owner*, tripped over in its excitement.

5. Jamie Oliver, *<u>mixing</u> the ingredients energetically into the curry*, enthusiastically prepared the meal, which was to be served to many celebrities.

6. The Cotswold mansion, *<u>run down</u> by tenants whose only aim was to avoid spending money*, was in need of major repairs.

7. The mountain bike, *<u>skidding</u> at breakneck speed down the hillside*, crashed on to the mountain road, causing a traffic accident.

EXTENSION

Rewrite and improve the variety of the sentences, by moving the **prepositional phrases** in italics to a different position in each sentence.

1. Exeter University is located *near to the sea*.

2. The legal document that she needed lay *on the desk beneath a pile of papers*.

3. The mobile phone for which you have been searching is *inside the glove compartment*.

4. The old warehouse whose windows and doors had been broken was *at the end of the street*.

5. Squadrons of aircraft, which were capable of destroying the tanks, were based *at the front line*.

6. The Glastonbury festival throbbed to the music *under a canopy of stars*.

7. The setting sun is *beyond the western edge of Europe*.

SENTENCE VARIETY 3

If the same pattern or rhythm is used in a series of sentences, look at ways of improving the **variety** of the sentences by:

* using clauses and phrases with **indicator words** such as *after, although, as, because, before, even though, if only, rather than, since, wherever* at the beginning of some sentences

* varying the rhythm of sentences by adding **transition words** such as *accordingly, after all, also, consequently, however, in conclusion, in the meantime, in the same way, meanwhile, moreover, nevertheless* at the beginning of some sentences

* varying the rhythm of the writing by **using some short sentences and some long ones**, eg

    We visited Israel and Egypt one summer, while on holiday in Cyprus. Regular cruises sailed from Limassol. Although we visited each country only for a day, we were able to see Bethlehem, Jerusalem and the pyramids at Gizeh. It was wonderful.

On the flight deck of the aircraft carrier a Sea Harrier was getting ready for takeoff.

FOCUS

Rewrite the following sentences by placing the underlined **indicator words** at the beginning, after which you may need to change the word order.

1. A Sea Harrier was getting ready for takeoff <u>on the flight deck of the aircraft carrier</u>.
2. I <u>hardly ever</u> exercise in the evenings.
3. His parents <u>hardly ever</u> arrived late to pick him up.
4. I would <u>not</u> let my friends down <u>for all the money in the world</u>.
5. The employees knew <u>little</u> that the company would be closed down.
6. We would <u>not</u> sell our DVDs <u>for anything</u>.

INVESTIGATION

Rewrite and improve the variety of the sentences, by adding **transition words** to each pair.

1. The boys were throwing stones. Windows were broken in a neighbouring house.
2. Nina was doing the Christmas shopping. I was browsing in the bookshop.
3. It was a long drive to Oxford. I decided that Charlie needed me to be there.
4. John advised me to revise the manuscript. I made the changes he recommended.
5. I decided to have the garden landscaped. It would make access easier.

EXTENSION

Rewrite and improve the variety of the passage, by **using some long and some short sentences**. Join some sentences and use **transition words**.

Our neighbours were noisy. They got on my dad's nerves. There were four children. They had three boys and a girl. They played bad music loudly. They ran up and down the stairs. They did not cut the hedge that bordered our shared path. They behaved aggressively towards us. They shouted abuse and threatened us.

SENTENCE BEGINNINGS 1

Varying your sentence patterns helps you to keep your reader's interest. Knowing how to use different sentence patterns allows you to choose the one best suited to your purpose. One simple way to improve the variety of sentences is to change the **beginnings**. Begin with:

- one or more **modifiers (modifying words)** – these can be **adjectives** or **adverbs**, eg

  Huge, ugly and scarred, the thug blocked the alley.

- a **prepositional phrase**, eg

  In the hectic business of cooking for twenty children, Mrs Pickwick excelled.

- **more than one prepositional phrase**, eg

  On this particular occasion, *above all other occasions*, the embarrassment proved too much.

- a **modifying adjectival** or **adverbial clause**, eg

  When young men learn bad ways, they are sure to come to bad ends.

- a **noun clause**, eg

  What was meant by this comment the victim never knew, for his life came to an abrupt end.

As soon as school ends, I will meet you at the bus stop.

FOCUS

Copy and rewrite each sentence to make it begin with a **one-word modifier**, a **phrase** or a **clause**.

1 I will meet you at the bus stop as soon as school ends.
2 The bus usually responds to requests to pick up passengers.
3 I allowed plenty of time to be sure of getting to the interview.
4 I ask my daughters to help with the cooking and tidying up when we have friends to dinner.
5 I often have difficulty with mathematics and science.
6 We watched fireflies at the caravan site in France.

INVESTIGATION

On a separate sheet of paper, rewrite each sentence, filling in the blank to make it begin with a **one-word modifier**, a **phrase**, or a **clause**.

1 _____, I'm disappointed in Damien's insolent attitude.
2 _____ the hotel bathroom didn't have any air conditioning to regulate the temperature.
3 _____, Yolandee won an academic prize for English.
4 _____, we found the hotel car park.
5 _____ the eccentric artist usually swam in the lake.
6 _____, we should wash our hands.
7 _____ she always seems irritable.
8 _____, there are many homeless people.
9 _____, we knew we would see her again soon.
10 _____ is that she has been seeing someone else.

EXTENSION

On a separate sheet of paper, rewrite each of the following sentences according to the instructions in brackets. You will need to add an adjective, adverb, participle, phrase or clause of your own. You may need to move, change or delete words, and change punctuation where necessary.

1 _____ Hannah followed George to Barcelona. (adjective first)
2 _____Hannah followed George to Barcelona. (adverb first)
3 _____ Chloe accompanied George to Spain. (participle first)
4 ____ Chloe accompanied George to Spain. (prepositional phrase first)
5 _____ Hannah wanted to have a relationship with George. (adverbial clause first)

SENTENCE BEGINNINGS 2

In Topic 21, we looked at some of the basic ways of beginning sentences. There are other ways that you can start sentences. You can begin with:

- an **infinitive phrase**

  An infinitive looks like a verb (eg *to be*, *to hold*), but it is a noun and it can be the subject of a clause or the object of a verb. An infinitive phrase is made up of the infinitive and the word(s) that go with it, eg

    *She wanted **to stay behind**.*

    infinitive   accompanying word

    infinitive phrase

- a **gerund**, which is a type of verb that ends in *-ing* but acts as if it was a noun, eg

    *My favourite pastime is **reading**.*

    gerund

Becky wants to play football when she grows up.

FOCUS

Copy and complete each of the following sentences using a suitable **infinitive** or **infinitive phrase**.

1 Becky wants _____ when she grows up.
2 _____ is the desire of most people.
3 _____ my father, you have to live with him for a month.
4 A good way to get what you want is _____ assertively.
5 It is important _____ your hands before dinner.
6 The decision _____ a house is never easy.
7 _____ a life sentence must seem like a nightmare.

INVESTIGATION

Copy and complete each of the following sentences, by using a suitable **gerund**. The first one has been done for you.

1 _____ is everyone's greatest concern.
   Staying healthy is everyone's greatest concern.
2 _____ is a sure way to provoke an argument.
3 One of Estelle's favourite pastimes is _____ the piano.
4 I hate _____ my hair but my girlfriend makes me.
5 Gerard felt like _____ cake before _____ dinner.
6 _____ to the Caribbean for a holiday is a dream that most people do not achieve.
7 _____ the driving test, she needs to improve her roadcraft.
8 _____ a new college is quite stressful as well as exciting.

EXTENSION

Rewrite the following sentences into one paragraph. Join sentences and use a variety of sentence structures.

William Shakespeare was a great writer.

He was a soldier and a producer, as well.

He was born in Stratford-upon-Avon.

He married a woman older than himself.

They had several children.

For several years, he disappeared.

No one knows what he was doing during those years.

He reappeared in London as an actor.

He became part-owner of the Globe Theatre.

He wrote many famous plays and poems.

SENTENCE TRANSITIONS

Transitions help you to connect the ideas contained in a piece of writing. They show how the parts of your text fit together. Sometimes all you have to do is put in a **transition cue**, which is a word or phrase that helps to guide readers through the text. There are various types of transition cue:

- cues that lead you forward from information you've already read to **new information**, or that **develop your ideas** or move you into **specific examples**, eg

  *actually   additionally   besides   equally important
  further   incidentally   indeed   moreover
  what's more   as an illustration*

- cues that lead you through a **sequence**, especially ones that move you from one **place** or **time-frame** to another, eg

  Place: *alongside   in the distance   near by   adjacent*

  Time: *afterwards   at last   at the same time   during
  eventually   finally   formerly   initially
  in the meantime   later   previously   subsequently*

- cues that draw your attention to **cause and effect** relationships or to the **purpose**, eg

  Cause: *as   for   because   due to   since*

  Effect: *as a result   for this reason   so
  consequently   therefore   thus*

  Purpose: *so that   in the hope that   in order to
  with this in mind*

- cues that make you stop and **compare** what you've just read to what you're about to read, eg

  *although   at the same time   conversely   in comparison
  still   nevertheless   similarly   however   on the contrary
  likewise   on the other hand   while this is true   whereas*

Incidentally, did you hear the one about the Four Musketeers?   Specific example

FOCUS

Copy the sentences and underline the **transition cues**. Say what type of transition cue they are.

1 Incidentally, did you hear the one about the Four Musketeers?
2 In order to present the next example, I will point the ruler.
3 Due to leaves on the line, the train is cancelled.
4 Since you cannot be polite, you had better say nothing.
5 Alongside, the sailor was mooring his dinghy.
6 Initially, I had no enthusiasm for the food.

INVESTIGATION

Cues leading to statements that **clarify** a point that you have just read or that **emphasise** a point you are about to read are:

Clarify: *in other words   in this case   put another way*

Emphasise: *indeed   undoubtedly   as a matter of fact*

On a separate sheet of paper, write six sentences of your own. Begin three sentences with **transitions to clarify** and three sentences with **transitions to emphasise**.

1 _____
2 _____
3 _____
4 _____
5 _____
6 _____

EXTENSION

Cues leading to a **summary** or **conclusion** are:

Summary: *briefly   finally   in short   on the whole   overall*
therefore   summing up   in summary

Conclusion: *accordingly   as a result   consequently*
hence   in conclusion   to conclude

On a separate sheet of paper, write four sentences of your own. Begin two sentences with **transitions to summarise** and two sentences with **transitions to conclude**.

1 _____
2 _____
3 _____
4 _____

CHECK-UP 2

Simple and compound sentences

Copy the sentences and tick the Simple column if the sentence is **simple**, or the Compound one if it is **compound**.

	Simple	Compound
1 We bought tickets to the England rugby game.		
2 We sat toward the middle of the Twickenham stadium.		
3 Rugby is a physical game and the crowd roars in support.		
4 Rugby players are tough but they can get hurt frequently.		
5 The scrum half on each team stays near the pack.		
6 Rugby players obey the referee or they regret it.		
7 Rugby is a popular sport in many countries around the world.		
8 Rugby players move quickly or they will be tackled.		

Complex sentences

Copy the sentences and complete them by adding a subordinate clause of your own.

1 I argued _____.

2 The pupil _____ was given a detention.

3 _____ I was delighted.

4 _____ I like to go snowboarding.

5 The police came into the school _____.

Double negatives

Copy and correct the use of **double negatives** in the sentences.

1 Jefferson never cooks nothing interesting for dinner.

2 His daughters can't hardly wait for an improvement in their diet.

3 Jeff hasn't been reading no recipe books on how to cook badly, has he?

4 Veronica did not feel nothing when she had an accident.

5 She doesn't know no one at the hospital.

6 Veronica used to play volleyball but she doesn't no more.

Active and passive voice

Copy and complete the sentences by choosing the correct form of the verb from the two versions given in brackets.

1 Dr Golby _____ at Exeter University since the 1980s.

   (has been teaching/has been taught)

2 He _____ the girl's telephone number if he fancies her.

   (remembers/is remembered)

3 A new book _____ by Nelson Thornes next year.

   (will publish/will be published)

4 The secretary _____ to her new boss yesterday.

   (introduced/was introduced)

5 A prize _____ to whoever solves this puzzle.

   (will be giving/will be given)

Sentence variety

Copy the sentences and complete them according to the instructions.

1 Add a **modifier** to the **beginning** of this sentence:

   _____ the hurricane howled across the city.

2 Add a **modifier** to the **middle** of the sentence:

   The dog _____ rolled in the manure.

3 Add a **modifier** to the **end** of this sentence:

   The computer crashed _____.

4 Add **modifiers** to the **beginning and the end** of this sentence:

   _____ the teenagers pointed _____.

5 Add **modifiers** to the **middle and the end** of this sentence:

   The pensioner _____ chased the mugger _____.

Sentence beginnings

Copy the sentences and complete them according to the instructions.

1 Add a **modifying adjective** and a **modifying adverb** to the beginning of the sentence.

   _____ the bullies terrorised their victims.

2 Add a **prepositional phrase** to the beginning of the sentence.

   _____ the headteacher excelled.

3 Add a **modifying adjectival** or **adverbial clause** to the beginning of the sentence.

   _____ they are certain to do well.

4 Add a **noun clause** to the beginning of the sentence.

   _____ because the film had a 'cliff-hanger' ending.

PARA

Paragra   ntences that have the same topic
or main   aph must have three parts:

- **topic**   sually the first sentence.
  It giv   information in the paragraph.

- **body**   are the middle part of the paragraph.
  In the   back up the ideas that you introduced
  in the   the strongest point first, before giving
  other e

- **link/tr**   he last sentence of the paragraph.
  It shoul   **ransition** into the next paragraph,
  giving a   come.

Key word

Key word   the topic sentences and link/transition
sentences.   ce, these words show the reader what
your topic i   tion, they show what the next topic
will be, eg

Essay title: Storm at Sea

Paragraph   alm before the storm

Paragraph 2:   the build-up to the storm

Topic sentence 1:   It was a calm, still evening as the ship
                    nosed out of the harbour.

Key words: **calm**, **still** (main idea)
                    ship, **harbour** (background information)

Link/transition: The **quiet** evening began to give way to
                    rising winds and **looming storm-clouds**.

Topic sentence 2:   Clouds swept **stormily** towards the ship,
                    promising a **rough** voyage.

Forest Fire

FOCUS

Using the example above to help you, write one **topic sentence** and one **link/transition** sentence for a paragraph on each of the following subjects.

1 Forest Fire 2 The Teenage Party 3 The Windy Night

INVESTIGATION

Choose one of the subjects with its topic and link/transition sentences from the work you have just done in the Focus section, and build up a full paragraph by adding four **body sentences**. Use the following questions to help you plan your body sentences:

- Who or what is doing something?
- What is the person or thing doing?
- When is it happening?
- Where is it happening?
- How was or will it be done?

Try to put your body sentences in order of importance in the paragraph.

HINT

Body sentences develop the ideas introduced by the topic sentence.

EXTENSION

Each of these paragraphs contains one sentence that does not really belong in it. Copy the paragraphs and underline that sentence.

1 Dear Rose, how are you? I'm interested to know how you're getting on. How is El? Has she acquired many new friends? I have a new car. Tell me about your new house; is it as pretty as your old one? Are you glad you moved? Do you miss me?

2 Michael is a collector. He has an extensive collection of vintage tractors. His collection of model trains is his latest obsession. The art collection that decorates his walls is a mixture of paintings and reliefs. Michael loves to vacuum the house. He has a collection of Massey Ferguson memorabilia, a comic book collection of designers' work, and even a collection of folk music. It's no wonder that Michael's friends call him 'The Collector'.

3 Laurence was not as popular with her teachers as she was with her peers. She knew that she had earned the teachers' dislike and disapproval. She laughed aloud when Mr Burkitt made serious comments in class. She drew ugly cartoons of Mrs Barratt and stuck them on the classroom notice board. Her favourite subject was art. Every day, in every class, Laurence just complained, "When can I leave this school?"

PARAGRAPHS 2

<u>All paragraphs need a clear beginning, a middle and an end.</u> The beginning is the topic sentence which says what the paragraph is about. The middle will be several sentences that explain, or give examples, or prove the topic sentence. The end will be the final sentence, which will sum up the paragraph or link it to the topic in the next paragraph. <u>In this way, a paragraph is clearly organised.</u>

The **paragraph** above is clearly organised. The **topic sentence** is underlined and so is the **link/transition** sentence that sums up the whole paragraph. It restates the main idea. The three **body sentences** in the middle explain or develop the idea from the topic sentence.

Look at this paragraph:

> *British troops suffered <u>heavy casualties</u> in the American War of Independence because of their <u>red coats</u>. The American rebels were fighting for their own homes and so fought with total commitment. The American generals were more creative than the British and fought with great skill. The <u>scarlet uniforms</u> of the British army made them easy targets for the skilled American marksmen. In this way the traditional <u>uniform</u> of the British soldiers contributed to their own <u>defeat</u>.*

The paragraph's subject is stated clearly in the topic sentence and is restated in the link/transition sentence. However, the second and third sentences have nothing to do with the British uniforms and should not be in the paragraph. **Key words** have been underlined to show how they are restated.

The Ferrari is the most powerful production car in the world.

FOCUS

Use each of the **topic sentences** below to begin writing paragraphs of your own. Remember that all the sentences must be related to the topic stated in the sentence given. Use **key words** and **transition cues**.

1 The Ferrari is the most powerful production car in the world.
2 Dad's mood that day was particularly foul.
3 There was an eerie, menacing atmosphere about the place.
4 As the valley mist cleared, a scene of spectacular beauty emerged.
5 Everything about the man's expression showed a vicious nature.

INVESTIGATION

Write a paragraph on the subject 'The Excited Crowd'. It should have a clear **topic sentence**, **body sentences** and a **link/transition** sentence. Use **key words** and **transition cues**.

Here are some words to help give you ideas:

songs   chants   banners   streamers

scarves   placards   colour   old people

young people   dancing   delight   throbbing

swaying   pushing   jostling   urgent   riot

sounds   exploding   wild   time

EXTENSION

Write a second paragraph of your own to follow the one above on 'The Excited Crowd'. You will need to decide:

- what the **topic** of the second paragraph will be
- a **topic sentence** to begin the paragraph
- which **key words** from the **link/transition sentence** of the first paragraph will be restated in the **topic sentence** of the second paragraph
- the **body sentences** that will explain, give examples, or prove the topic
- what you want to say in your last sentence to **conclude** the paragraph

PARAGRAPHS 3

Once you can create suitable paragraphs, you will develop longer pieces of writing. In school, these longer pieces will often be called **essays**. Essays are just like paragraphs because they need a beginning, a middle and a conclusion.

Introduction

Essays always start with an **introduction**. For a good introduction you need to:

- interpret the question or title of the essay
- show how you are going to answer the question

You can do this by:

- using the words and phrases of the question or title
- showing you know what issues these words and phrases suggest
- indicating the main areas that will be covered in your essay
- making sure that all sentences are linked directly to the question or title

To write a good introduction, you need to follow these steps:

1. Write a clear **topic sentence**.

2. In the **body sentences** use active voice for a direct, purposeful style – do not waffle – and give evidence for the points you put forward.

3. End with a strong **link/transition** sentence.

The Old Church

FOCUS

Write a plan for a three-paragraph description entitled 'The Old Church'. For paragraph 1, decide on the **topic sentences** for the **introduction**. For paragraph 2, give some examples for the **body sentences** of the description. Write down your ideas for **concluding** the description in paragraph 3.

INVESTIGATION

To prepare for the writing of the description that you have planned, use a dictionary to research and write down the meaning of the words in the list.

1 *repulsive*
2 *decrepit*
3 *crumbling*
4 *ramshackle*
5 *decaying*
6 *verminous*
7 *nauseating*
8 *dilapidated*

Use a thesaurus to find four more words that could describe an old church. Write down each word and its meaning.

EXTENSION

Write the introductory paragraph for the description entitled 'The Old Church'. It will need a clear **topic sentence**. Then, you must follow this with several **body sentences** to illustrate the topic. Finally, the paragraph must end with a **link/transition sentence** that restates the topic and connects to the next paragraph.

Paragraph 1 – Introduction
Topic sentence
Body sentence 1
Body sentence 2
Body sentence 3
Link/transition sentence

HINT

Remember to use key words in the topic sentence and in the link/transition sentence.

PARAGRAPHS 4

Opening sentences

When you are writing an essay or a longer piece of writing, you need to be able to grab your reader's attention and then maintain it throughout the piece. One effective technique for achieving this is to **dramatise the opening sentence** of your essay.

If you were writing an essay concerning the use of animals in medical research, one of the paragraph topics might be that cruelty to animals debases the people who carry it out. Therefore, the topic sentence could be:

This paragraph is about how animal cruelty debases the people that carry it out.

However, you can make this sentence much more effective by making it more dramatic, eg

- *It is depressing that civilised man should seek to make progress in medicine by inflicting terror, mutilation, agony and a horrible, tormented death on a fellow creature.*

- *Even the rats we slice up and mangle would never act as we do.*

- *Does man not lose something when he turns his genius and his most sophisticated machines to tearing animals to pieces?*

- *Must we always leave a trail of blood?*

As opening sentences, any of these would have an immediate impact on the reader. Once you have the reader's attention you explain yourself in the body of the paragraph. You follow up this dramatic, or exaggerated, opening sentence with details that show what you mean.

Man's greed causes pollution.

FOCUS

Below are some topic sentences. Rewrite each one so that it becomes a **dramatic opening sentence**.

1 This paragraph is going to be about how man's greed causes pollution.

2 This paragraph is going to be about the idiotic violence of hooligans.

3 This paragraph is going to be about how newspapers are most interested in sensational stories.

4 This paragraph is going to be about how drunk drivers cost lives.

5 This paragraph is going to be about how some people are more concerned about animals than they are about children.

INVESTIGATION

Choose one of the topics from the Focus section and write a complete **paragraph**. Concentrate on creating a clear **topic sentence**, **body sentences** and a **link/transition sentence**, using the framework below to help you.

Paragraph Topic

Key words

Topic sentence

Body sentence 1

Body sentence 2

Body sentence 3

Link/transition sentence

> *HINT*
>
> Remember to use key words in your topic and link/transition sentences.

EXTENSION

Choose a second topic from the Focus section and write a complete paragraph, beginning with a **dramatic opening sentence**. Use the framework below to help you.

Paragraph Topic

Key words

Topic sentence

Body sentence 1

Body sentence 2

Body sentence 3

Link/transition sentence

THE BASIC ESSAY: FLOW DIAGRAM

Preparation and planning are needed before starting to write a piece of three or more paragraphs. There are two main ways to plan an essay or longer piece of writing:

- the **flow diagram**, or mind map, tries to illustrate the flow of the writer's ideas

- the **outline** tries to structure the ideas to show how some are more important than others

The flow diagram

To make a flow diagram, start by writing the main topic of the essay in the middle of the page. Next, draw lines radiating out from the central topic. At the ends of the lines, write down the main ideas of the central topic. Then draw more lines radiating out from each of the main ideas. At the end of each of these lines, write down further information that relates to that particular main idea (*see* illustration).

This preparation and planning helps to give the essay a sense of the flow of points from one idea to another.

The flow diagram approach to preparing and planning is neither better nor worse than using the outline – they are just different ways of doing the same thing.

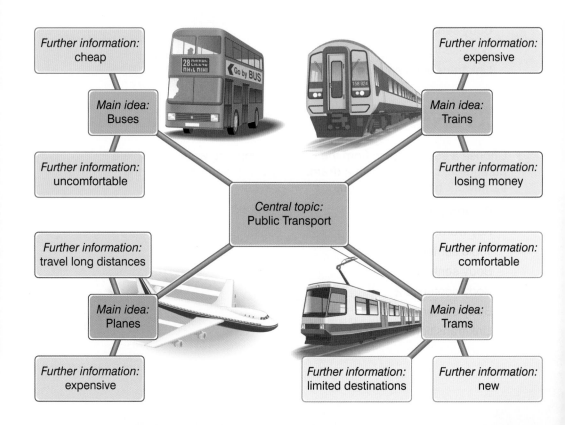

Further information: cheap

Main idea: Buses

Further information: uncomfortable

Further information: expensive

Main idea: Trains

Further information: losing money

Central topic: Public Transport

Further information: travel long distances

Further information: comfortable

Main idea: Planes

Main idea: Trams

Further information: expensive

Further information: limited destinations

Further information: new

FOCUS

Make a **flow diagram** of your own on the central topic 'Teenage Pregnancy', using the illustration opposite to help you. Include four main ideas, but do not put in the further information for each of those main ideas at this stage. Lay out your flow diagram in the same way as the illustration, but leave the further information boxes blank.

INVESTIGATION

Choose one of the main ideas from the flow diagram you made in the Focus section, eg *single parent*. Now draw a second **flow diagram** showing the information and ideas that you would include for that main idea, as shown below:

Information 4		Information 1
_____		_____
_____		_____
_____		_____
_____		_____
	Single parent	
Information 3		Information 2
_____		_____
_____		_____
_____		_____
_____		_____

EXTENSION

Taking your second flow diagram, write the **topic sentence** that would begin a paragraph on its main subject.

Then write the **link/transition sentence** that would end that same paragraph.

THE BASIC ESSAY: OUTLINE

The outline

In this method, you use the central topic of the essay, eg 'Public Transport in England', as the heading. Underneath, write the Roman numbers I, II and III, spaced out down a page. Next to each number, write down a main idea. Under each number, write A, B and C, spaced out down the page, then next to each letter put the ideas related to that particular main subject (*see* illustration).

This preparation and planning helps to give the essay a clear feeling of organisation and direction.

The outline approach to preparing and planning is neither better nor worse than using the flow diagram; which method you choose is a matter of personal preference.

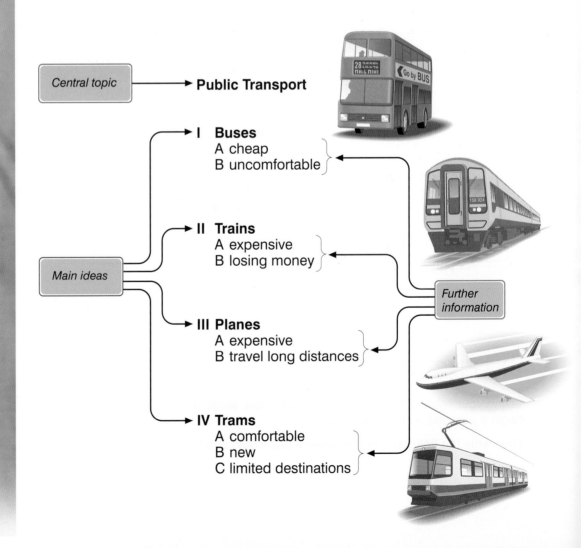

Central topic → **Public Transport**

Main ideas

I Buses
A cheap
B uncomfortable

II Trains
A expensive
B losing money

III Planes
A expensive
B travel long distances

IV Trams
A comfortable
B new
C limited destinations

Further information

FOCUS

Make an **outline** plan of your own on the central topic 'How Teenagers Use Their Time', using the illustration opposite to help you. Include four main ideas under the numbers I to IV, but do not include the further information under A, B and C at this stage. Lay out your outline in the same way as the illustration, but leave A, B and C blank.

INVESTIGATION

Choose one of the main ideas from your **outline** plan for the essay on 'How Teenagers Use Their Time'. Now plan the further information and ideas that you would include for that main subject, using the layout below to help you.

Main idea _____

A _____

_____

_____

B _____

_____

_____

C_____

_____

_____

EXTENSION

Take the main idea that you planned in the Investigation section. Write the **topic sentence** that would begin the first paragraph under this main idea.

Then write the **link/transition sentence** that would end the first paragraph.

THE BASIC ESSAY: INTRODUCTION

After the initial planning, there are two stages involved in beginning to write an essay:

- you have to grab the reader's attention

- once you have the reader's attention, you need to make clear your approach to the subject that you are writing about. This is sometimes called **defining your thesis**.

Your approach (thesis)

When setting out to deal with a central topic, eg Public Transport in England, you will need to decide what your **approach** will be. The approach that you take to an essay may be serious, it may be light-hearted, it may be favourable or it may be critical. When you are clear about the approach that you want to take, you can then decide on the type of introduction that you want to write.

Usually the last sentence of an introduction states clearly your argument and the approach that you are taking to the subject:

- state the **topic**: Public Transport in England

- state the **point** of the essay:
  – is collapsing because of government policy
  – can solve congestion on the roads
  – is an unpleasant way to travel

You Can't Choose Your Relatives

Beginning your introduction

1 Give the reader **surprising information**, eg *At the beginning of the 20th century, cars had to be preceded by a man with a red flag, to warn the public of their approach!*

2 Tell the reader an **interesting story**, eg *My great-uncle was the first man in England to be killed by public transport; he was run over by a tram!*

3 Begin with two or three sentences of **dialogue**, eg *'Did you hear about the train accident, yesterday?' 'Yes, my baby-sitter was burned to death.'*

4 Give **summary information**, explaining the central topic and the point of the essay (thesis), eg *Public transport in England has been the subject of much controversy recently. I believe that a good public transport system could reduce congestion on the roads.*

5 **Jump straight in** to the central topic, eg *Public transport in England is in a terrible state!*

6 Start with a **specific image**, eg *I could not believe my eyes when I saw that the plane I was about to board had a logo of a naked woman!*

7 Introduce something **mysterious**, eg *The train halted in the midnight darkness, yet there did not seem to be a station, nor any reason for the delay.*

8 Start with a **problem**, eg *Public transport is costing every taxpayer a great deal of money, yet the system continues to fail. What is to be done?*

End your introduction with a link/transition sentence that restates the approach (thesis).

FOCUS

On a separate sheet of paper, write your own **thesis**, using only two sentences, on the central topic 'You Can Choose Your Friends But You Can't Choose Your Relatives'.

State the **topic**:_____

State the **point** of the essay: _____

INVESTIGATION

Complete either a **flow diagram** or an **outline** plan for a basic essay of several paragraphs on the central topic 'You Can Choose Your Friends But You Can't Choose Your Relatives'.

EXTENSION

Write the opening sentence for the central topic 'You Can Choose Your Friends But You Can't Choose Your Relatives' using each of the eight types of **introduction** above.

THE BASIC ESSAY: BODY PARAGRAPHS

Body paragraphs explain, describe or argue the writer's **approach (thesis)** to the central topic. Each main idea from the flow diagram or outline plan becomes one of the body paragraphs.

Organising a body paragraph

- Begin the body paragraph with a **topic sentence**.

- Write down, in sentence form, each of the points of information or ideas that are linked to the **main idea**. Leave several lines of space in between each point.

- In the space under each point write a sentence explaining that point in more detail, or giving examples to support it.

- Write a **link/transition sentence** that restates the main idea and links this body paragraph to the next one.

Improving body paragraphs

- **Prioritise** the points of information and examples given in support of the topic sentence. Some points will be more important than others. Put the strongest points first.

- Make the reader's **progress** through the body paragraphs clear. The points you explain in the first body paragraphs should lead on sensibly to the following body paragraphs.

- **Paint a vivid picture** in your writing. Use **nouns** to help the reader to see what your point is, and **verbs** to help them to share your feelings about it. Images, such as **metaphors** and **similes** can give your writing impact.

On the roof of the shed

FOCUS

Copy the passage. Underline the sentences which do <u>not</u> develop the main idea revealed in the **topic sentence**.

> When I was growing up, one of the places that I liked to use as an escape from my family was the roof of the shed. On the other side of the shed was a neighbour's garden. Every summer evening when it was warm and quiet, I'd climb to the ridge of the shed. My mother was anxious that I might fall and injure myself but I never did. Once up on the roof, I was able to bask in the last, balmy rays of the setting sun, relaxing and gaining some peace of mind. It was a haven of tranquillity.

INVESTIGATION

Copy the following **topic** and **link/transition sentences**. In the gaps, add three sentences that **develop the main idea**. Every sentence that you add must support the main idea with information, explanation, example or evidence.

1 Rugby Union was traditionally the game of the upper-class, privately educated man. (a) _____
   (b) _____ (c) _____
   Today, England's rugby team is followed enthusiastically by families from all sectors of society, not just the privileged.

2 When The Beatles first appeared, the older generation regarded them as a threat to civilised society. (a) _____
   (b) _____ (c) _____
   Nowadays, many in Britain look on The Beatles as a valued part of the musical history of the nation.

EXTENSION

Rewrite the passage, changing the order of the sentences so that the paragraph begins with a **topic sentence**, **develops a body of information** and ends with a **link/transition sentence**.

> It was here that I learned much of the world at large; of terrifying bullies trying to burn me with cigarettes; of an impatient older generation with no tolerance for boys. I lived near the River Thames – a place of endless interest. In the dense, impoverished bushes, we made our dens; places of secret fumings of wicked cigarettes and erotic fumblings. Its attraction was its continuous stream of people, activities and events to entertain and educate a young boy. From the gravel pits, steep-sided and dangerous, to the slow-flowing river, there was always some watery diversion to occupy me.
>
> Yet, whether the experiences were painful or joyful, there was never a dull moment near the river. Then, there were the scrubby bush-lands of the no-mans-land between the prefab council estates and the tow-path.

THE BASIC ESSAY: CONCLUSION

The **conclusion** sums up the point of the essay (**thesis**), giving a final definite view on the **central topic**. The first sentence of the conclusion usually restates the thesis of the essay. The information is specific to the central topic, often summarising the paragraphs from the body of the essay. Then the conclusion ends by making general points, often trying to make the essay and its ideas universal. The conclusion is not the place to bring up new ideas; instead, it is intended to leave the reader with a lasting impression.

Aims of the conclusion

- to signal to the reader that the essay is finished
- no new material should be introduced
- to explain consequences or implications and emphasise your point
- to leave the reader with a fresh view of the main ideas
- to show how the main ideas relate to the central topic
- to refer back to the introduction but relate your ideas to broader issues
- to give a sense of closure to the essay's organisation

Useful phrases in writing a conclusion

If you are wanting to summarise: *In short ...   In a word ... In brief ...   To sum up ...*

If you are wanting to conclude: *In conclusion ...   On the whole ... Altogether ...   In all ...   Therefore it can be concluded that ... On this basis it may be deduced that ...   From the information it can be shown that ...   From the results it is seen that ...*

King Arthur – truth or fiction?

Techniques to conclude an essay

1 Ask a provocative or controversial **question**, eg

   Does the headteacher really think he can act like a dictator?

2 Use a **quotation**, eg

   'The only thing that I have to declare is my genius.'
   (Oscar Wilde, on arriving at Customs)

3 Produce a **vivid image**, eg

   The last I saw of her, as she slipped beneath the black waters, was a single hand clawing at the ice.

4 Call for **action** of some kind, eg

   Let us unite in the battle against poverty. Let us act – NOW!

5 End with a **warning**, eg

   If we do not reduce global warming, the ice-caps will melt and sea levels will rise, drowning London and New York.

6 **Compare** with other similar issues, eg

   The struggle for human rights in the 20th century mirrors the struggle to remove slavery in the 19th century.

7 Suggest the **results** or **consequences**, eg

   The result of American imperialism will be to further alienate the Muslims, the peoples of the southern hemisphere and all under-developed countries, which see the USA as the 'Great Satan'.

FOCUS

Rewrite and improve this concluding paragraph.

   To end my essay on King Arthur. Nobody knows much about him. No one knows who he was for sure. He was a hero, who fought the Saxons.

INVESTIGATION

Copy the following **thesis**:

   Subject: *Intelligent life in the universe*
   Point: *The universe is so vast, there must be intelligent life somewhere.*

Now write a whole **concluding paragraph** for an imaginary essay entitled 'Aliens are Alive and Well and Living Out There!' Be sure to use a **topic sentence**, several **body sentences** and a strong **concluding sentence**.

EXTENSION

Use the **concluding paragraph** you wrote in the Investigation section as the basis for a new **conclusion**. Use one of the seven techniques described above.

THE BASIC ESSAY: NARRATIVES

Many people like to use stories in their essays, especially if they are about personal enthusiasms or interests. Such stories are called **narratives** and readers often find them interesting and memorable.

Ways to tell a story (narrative), within an essay

- The **flash-forward** is used to show the progress or growth of an interest or ability. It starts the essay with the narrative of a recent event and then moves backwards in time to show how the interest or activity grew or progressed, eg

  Last week, I finally managed to pass my life-saving award. For many months, I had been struggling to build up my stamina ...

- The **book-end** begins the essay with the first part of a narrative but it leaves the end of the story until the **concluding paragraph** of the essay. The narrative breaks off while the writer discusses the impact of the experience. Here, the writer uses a flash-back technique, eg

  My story begins when my family was evicted from our rented home ... (**narrative** begins) *... The experience of being homeless was to affect me throughout my life ...* (essay diverts to reflect on that experience) *... Finally, we moved into the relative luxury of a council house ...* (**narrative** concludes)

- **Narrative in body** signals to the reader that a narrative is about to start. The writer does this by using an introductory phrase, eg

  One remarkable incident happened when ...

The writer must be making an important point at the end of this narrative, otherwise the story should not be included in the essay.

I cycled in the park.

FOCUS

Copy the sentences. Say whether the writer is using the **flash-forward**, **book-end** or **narrative-in-body** technique.

1   It all began one hot summer's day, as I cycled in the park. ...This experience proved to me that people are essentially good.

2   On Friday, I achieved my dream of winning an Oscar. The previous Thursday ...

3   In 1996, I decided that I wanted to be a farmer. ... By 2002, it was clear that my farming days were over.

INVESTIGATION

Copy the passage and explain which technique you think the writer has used. Write down the sentences in the passage that support your opinions.

One painful incident, which shows the folly of volunteering, happened when I was 12 years of age. During a PE lesson, the teacher decided to hold a series of wrestling matches between the boys. After two or three bouts, the number of volunteers dwindled, as we watched people getting hurt. The teacher began to look disappointed, so I put up my hand to volunteer. I was matched with Pete Brown, who was smaller but stockier than me.

We grappled in the centre of the mat, trying for a decisive hold. Moments later, I had Pete in a bear-hug and he had me in a head-lock. I lifted him off his feet but over-balanced and we both toppled over. Falling towards the mat, I put out my arm to cushion the impact. There was a sickening crack, as my arm failed to take the combined weight of the two bodies. The consequence of volunteering was a broken arm!

EXTENSION

Choose the **flash-forward**, **book-end** or **narrative-in-body** technique and then write your own narrative to fit into an essay on 'The Problems of Volunteering!'

STYLE

Writing **style** affects how your reader reacts. A direct style is not only more effective to read, but it is also more enjoyable. A point is most forceful when it is conveyed concisely and directly. Problems of style usually arise when writers try to include too many points into one sentence and use too many clauses.

Varying sentence constructions

To make each sentence sound fresh and new, a good piece of writing will vary its **sentence constructions** by:

- combining shorter sentences into compound sentences
- using prepositional phrases, and varying their positions
- using conjunctions, and varying their positions
- using participles and gerunds

Tips for a good style

- use short simple words
- use precise language
- use nouns and verbs rather than adverbs and adjectives
- avoid repetition
- avoid passive voice
- use active voice

I saw the girl look up...

FOCUS

Copy the sentences and simplify or vary their construction, so that their **style and tone** is improved.

1 I walked into the party. The girl looked up at me. I greeted her with a smile. Her eyes brightened.
(weak style – short, fragmented sentences)

I saw the girl look up as I entered the party. I tried to appear friendly and interested by greeting her with a smile. Her brightening eyes showed that she responded.
(better style – more varied sentence constructions)

2 The game had begun. Our view was blocked by a pillar.
3 I felt I had to concentrate. The exam would soon be over.
4 They faced many risks. They became illegal immigrants.
5 I started a new company. I had to do many different jobs.
6 The pupils ran to see the exam results that had been posted on the board.

INVESTIGATION

Copy the sentences and improve the **style** by changing them from the passive voice into the active voice.

1 He was given so many chances to start again by his girlfriend.
2 She was told to remain in her seat by her teacher.
3 Their plans were frustrated by the neighbours' objections.
4 The road repairs were started late by the contractors.
5 The door was slammed by the moody teenager.

> ## HINT
> Find the subject of the action (the noun that follows 'by') and bring that to the front of the clause. Remove the 'to be' verb. Change the word order if necessary.

EXTENSION

Copy the sentences and improve the **style** by changing the weak verbs for stronger, action verbs.

1 I had opportunities to improve my skills.
2 I got the promotion because of my dedication.
3 He did well in a competitive school.
4 My parents didn't want to go to the dinner party without flowers for the hostess.
5 The double-glazing salesman told the audience about the products.

> ## HINT
> Use strong action verbs. In addition to avoiding 'to be' verbs, try to change helping verbs ('have', 'had', 'has', 'do', 'does', 'did') and other weak verbs, eg 'get', 'got'.

STYLE DEVICES AND TONE

Style devices that writers use often rely on comparisons or associations between things.

- A **symbol** is a person, object, situation or action that represents or stands for something else, eg the heart is used to represent love.

- **Connotation** is the association of a word with a feeling or idea, eg red may be associated with blood, danger or passion.

- **Imagery** is the most widely used device and is the most important. It is used to create a setting or mood, or to describe a character or smell, sound or action.

- **Metaphors** and **similes** compare things that are not alike in most ways but are similar in one particular way. Metaphors state that something is something else; similes use the words *like* or *as* to connect the two things being compared, eg

  That girl is a cow, but that boy eats like a pig!
  　　　└─────┘　　　　　　　└─────────┘
  　　　metaphor　　　　　　　　simile

- **Personification** gives a human trait to a non-human being or inanimate object, eg *The waves **ran** up the beach.*

Tone reveals the writer's attitude towards the subject or sets a mood:

- **Onomatopoeia** is when words sound like their meanings, eg

  The birds chirped.

- **Alliteration** is the repetition of initial consonants, as in tongue-twisters, eg

  She sells sea-shells on the sea shore.

- **Assonance** is the repetition of similar vowel sounds within a phrase, eg

  The wind whispered wistfully.

After a hard day's work I slipped gratefully into the welcoming comfort of my bed.

FOCUS

Copy the sentences and underline the **style devices**. Say what kind of style device each one is.

1. After a hard day's work I slipped gratefully into the welcoming comfort of my bed.
2. The intense hatred I felt for him gnawed at my temper until I hit him.
3. My mobile phone beeped impatiently; a text message had arrived.
4. A cold bright moon beamed coolly down onto the quiet woodland.
5. Enraged by my resistance, the wind struck me with greater violence.
6. Raging over a terrified town, the hurricane battered our trembling home.

HINT

A bed cannot welcome anything or anybody. The metaphor is giving the impression that the writer is glad to be in bed.

INVESTIGATION

Copy the sentences. Underline and identify the **style devices**. The first one has been done for you.

1. Peter Piper picked a peck of pickled peppers.

   Peter Piper picked a peck of pickled peppers.
   Alliteration on the letter 'p'.

2. The raindrops dripped from the ceiling into the bucket.
3. Tamara's bedroom is a pig-sty.
4. It was raining cats and dogs.
5. He looked like a million pounds; green and creased.
6. My love is like a red, red rose.
7. The exams killed me.
8. The rain in Spain falls mainly in the plain.

EXTENSION

Write eight sentences of your own using the words below. Each sentence should include at least one **style device**. Explain what style devices you have used.

1. bed
2. bird
3. clouds
4. hair
5. kitten
6. love
7. rain
8. sun

CHECK-UP 3

Topic sentences

Copy each of the following short passages and underline the
topic sentences. Give reasons for your choice.

1 Whales, which are amongst the world's largest mammals,
may be divided into two main types. Toothed whales bite
and chew their food. Baleen whales are filter feeders without
teeth. Despite there being many varieties of whale, they all
fall into one or other of the two categories.

2 Some people may think that WWW stands for a wrestling society,
or a German car manufacturer. In fact, the letters represent the
Internet, otherwise known as the World Wide Web. These letters
have become the most common abbreviation in the world.
Millions of people use the abbreviation every day on their computers.

3 The Normans conquered Britain but they did not mix easily with the
Saxons. Their different language and customs prevented social ease,
adding insult to the injury of having been defeated. French language
and customs began to take a prominent role in Saxon life.

Link/transition sentences

On a separate sheet of paper, write **link/transition sentences** that would
join paragraphs on the following **main ideas**:

Main idea 1

Dogs are a man's best friend.

Link/transition sentence: _____

Main idea 2

Dogs are descended from wolves.

Main idea 1

Ghosts are the spirits of the uneasy dead!

Link/transition sentence: _____

Main idea 2

Ghosts do not really exist.

Main idea 1

Cars are the main example of boys' toys!

Link/transition sentence: _____

Main idea 2

Women are just as good at driving as men!

Writing a conclusion

Write a short sentence of your own to complete each of these phrases.

1 In short ...

2 In brief ...

3 To sum up ...

4 In conclusion ...

5 On the whole ...

6 Altogether ...

7 In all ...

8 Therefore it can be concluded that ...

9 From the information it can be shown that ...

10 From the results it is seen that ...

Style

A Write down these 'fancy' words in a list on the left-hand side
of your book. Use a dictionary to look up their meanings.
Next, find plain, simple words that could replace the 'fancy'
words and write them down on the right-hand side.

1 endeavour

2 impact

3 utilise

4 procure

5 terminate

6 commence

7 finalise

8 parameters

9 interface

10 prioritise

B Now write sentences of your own using each of those plain words.

C Rewrite the following sentences to make them clearer, replacing
any overused or clumsily phrased expressions.

1 She looked as pretty as a picture.

2 The bar-maid had a heart of gold.

3 The farmer was as brown as a berry and as fit as a fiddle.

4 That sort of stuff riles my parents. They get all stirred up when
I leave the house without telling them where I am headed for.

5 Ain't that hunk fit?

Nelson Thornes **Framework English**

Core Writing Scheme

Year 7

Non-Fiction
0-7487-6542-5

Fiction
0-7487-6541-7

Teacher's Guide
0-7487-6543-3

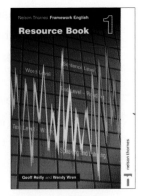

Resource Book
0-7487-6544-1

Year 8

Non-Fiction
0-7487-6948-X

Fiction
0-7487-6947-1

Teacher's Guide
0-7487-6949-8

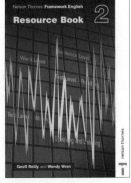

Resource Book
0-7487-6950-1

Year 9

Non-Fiction
0-7487-6952-8

Fiction
0-7487-6951-X

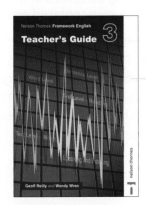

Teacher's Guide
0-7487-6953-6

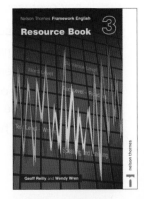

Resource Book
0-7487-6954-4